My First
Easy Words
Sticker Activity Book

This book belongs to

....

....

First published in 2015 by Scholastic Children's Books
Euston House, 24 Eversholt Street, London NW1 1DB
A division of Scholastic Ltd
www.scholastic.co.uk
Associated companies worldwide

Text copyright © 2015 Scholastic
Children's Books
Illustrations copyright © 2015 Jannie Ho

978 1407 14760 4

Printed in Malaysia
1 3 5 7 9 10 8 6 4 2

■SCHOLASTIC

At home

What's missing from the picture? Use the stickers to complete the house and garden.

tree

dog

indow

cat

door

3

Getting dressed

Colour in Alfie and Ava's outfits.

hat

coat

trousers

boots

dres

socks

shoes

Mealtime

Which path will lead Emily to the delicious apple?

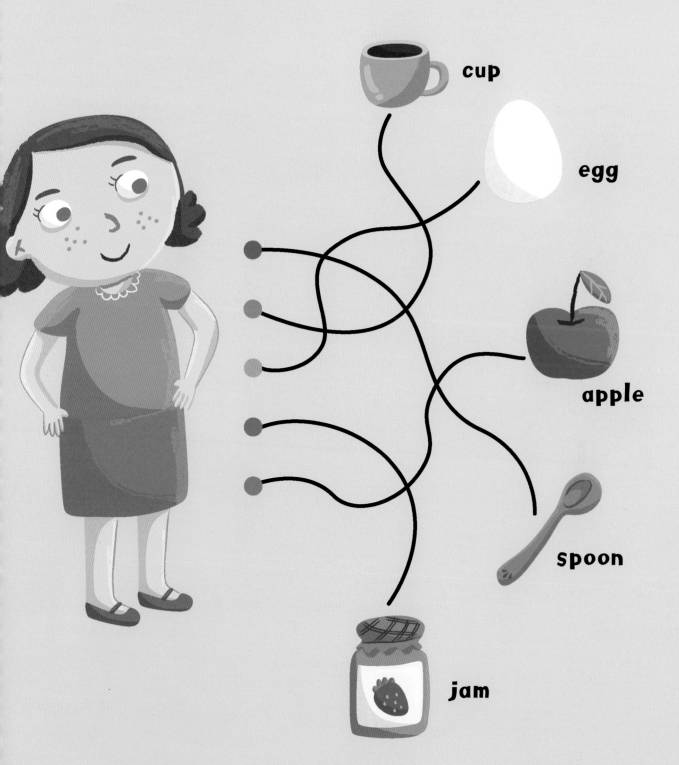

cup

egg

apple

spoon

jam

In the bedroom

Use the stickers to decorate Ben's bedroom.

teddy

lamp

book

ball

toy box

car

clock

rug

7

Let's go!

Beep, beep! Use the stickers to add lots of busy vehicles to the picture.

bus

bike

train

car

van

9

Opposites

Can you find the pairs? Join each word to its opposite.

wet

small

dry

hot

night

happy

cold

day

big

sad

TOYS

Use these stickers where you like

Colours

Use the stickers to find the matching object for each colour.

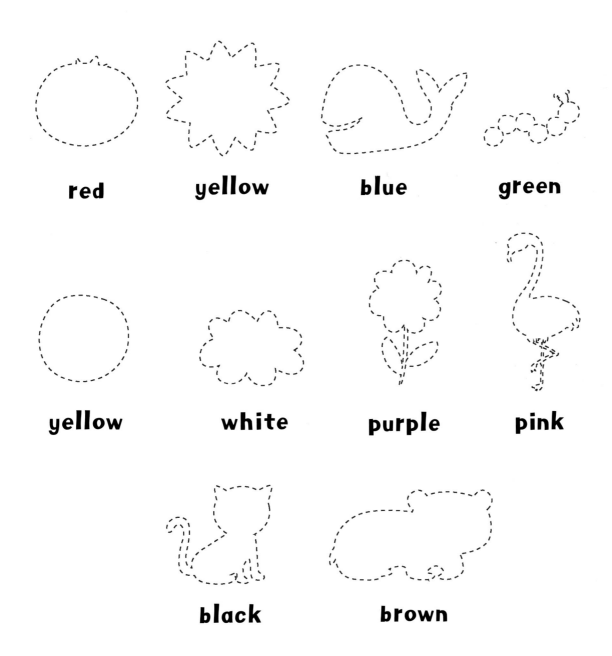

red   yellow   blue   green

yellow   white   purple   pink

black   brown

In the jungle

Colour in the jolly jungle animals.

monkey

elephant

snake

tiger

13

At the park

It's a sunny day in the park! Use the stickers to complete the picture.

bird

ball

girl

boy

tree

swings

flower

duck

15

Animal pairs

Can you match the baby animals with their mummies?

lamb

puppy

chick

kitten

cat

hen

sheep

dog

Seaside

Join the dots to draw a boat bobbing in the sea.

cloud

sun

boat

fish

beach

On the farm

Use the stickers to add lots of friendly animals to the farm.

cow

sheep

pig

horse

hen

19

Me!

Colour in the face and add some hair to the picture on this page.

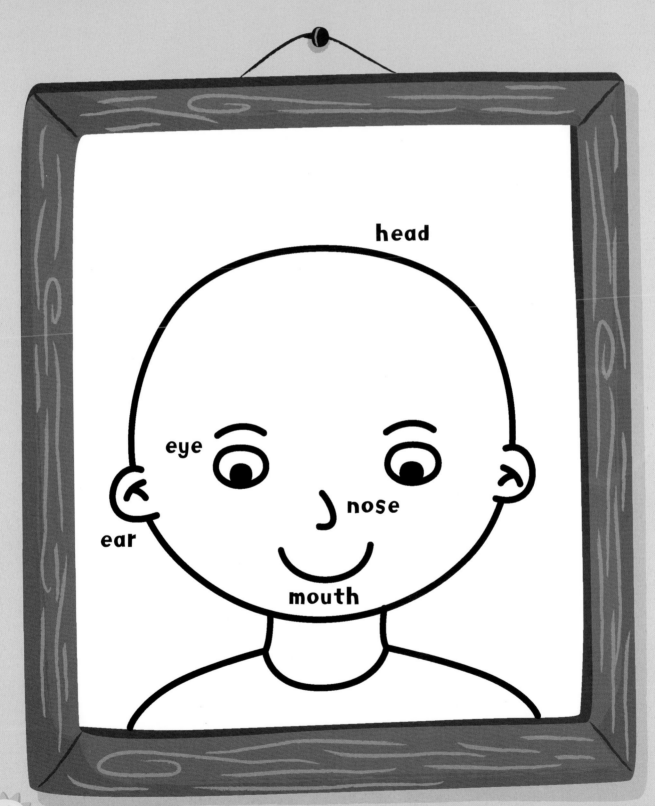